NATIONAL GALLERY OF ART · WASHINGTON · 1970

MARY CASSATT

1844-1926

EXHIBITION DATES:
National Gallery of Art
September 27, 1970 through November 8, 1970

Cover: No. 53, The Boating Party (detail)
Frontispiece: Photograph of Mary Cassatt, 1913 (Durand-Ruel)

Designed by Klaus Gemming, New Haven, Conn.
Composition by Finn Typographic Service, Stamford, Conn.
Printed in the United States of America
by The Meriden Gravure Company, Meriden, Conn.

Contents

Foreword

This exhibition of works by Mary Cassatt is the sixth in a continuing series organized by the National Gallery of Art to honor important American artists. Past exhibitions have been devoted to George Bellows, Winslow Homer, Thomas Eakins, John Singleton Copley, and, most recently, Gilbert Stuart.

Mary Cassatt differs from these five painters in two significant ways. First, obviously, she was a woman, in fact, America's greatest female artist. Second, she was one of a group of American artists, including Whistler and Sargent, who lived and worked abroad. Like them, she benefited from the extraordinary artistic developments occurring in Paris during the last quarter of the nineteenth century, particularly since Edgar Degas was her mentor. Yet she was able to absorb these influences and combine them with an inherent native quality which marks her work as distinctively American. As she herself insisted, "I am American . . . clearly and frankly American."

An exhibition of this scope would not be possible without the generous support of numerous museums and private collectors who were willing to lend us their pictures. This is particularly true of the private collectors, from which nearly two-thirds of the exhibition comes, who have made personal sacrifices in allowing their pictures to leave their walls. I extend my deepest appreciation to all the lenders for their cooperation, and particularly to the many members of the artist's family who have contributed so splendidly to the exhibition.

This exhibition would not have been possible without the assistance of Adelyn D. Breeskin, who helped us select the paintings and wrote the introduction and catalogue notes. For over twenty years Mrs. Breeskin, while pursuing a most distinguished museum career, has devoted herself to revealing the greatness of Mary Cassatt. Her research has resulted in numerous exhibition catalogues, articles, and the two essential books on the artist: *The Graphic Work of Mary Cassatt, a catalogue raisonné* and *Mary Cassatt: A Catalogue Raisonné of the Oils, Pastels, Watercolors, and Drawings*. The latter has just been published by the Smithsonian Institution Press and we are pleased that our exhibition coincides with the appearance of this definitive work.

I would like also to mention the helpful assistance of E. John Bullard, who has been the Gallery staff member specifically charged with the coordination of this show from its inception, and all those other members of the National Gallery staff whose labors have made this exhibition a reality.

J. Carter Brown
Director

Lenders

GORDON K. ALLISON, NEW YORK, NEW YORK

ANONYMOUS LENDERS

MRS. LESTER AVNET, NEW YORK, NEW YORK

MRS. DONALD B. BARROWS, BRYN MAWR, PENNSYLVANIA

MR. AND MRS. B. E. BENSINGER, CHICAGO, ILLINOIS

A. P. BERSOHN, NEW YORK, NEW YORK

PROF. DOROTHY BROWN, MALIBU, CALIFORNIA

ALEXANDER J. CASSATT, CECILTON, MARYLAND

MRS. GARDNER CASSATT, BRYN MAWR, PENNSYLVANIA

H. WENDELL CHERRY, LOUISVILLE, KENTUCKY

MR. AND MRS. DALE H. DORN, SAN ANTONIO, TEXAS

COLLECTION DURAND-RUEL, PARIS

MELVIN GELMAN COLLECTION, WASHINGTON

MRS. FLORENCE GOULD, CANNES

MR. AND MRS. WILLIAM H. GREEN, RIVER FOREST, ILLINOIS

DR. ARMAND HAMMER, LOS ANGELES, CALIFORNIA

CHARLES W. HARE, CAMBRIDGE, MASSACHUSETTS

HUNTINGTON HARTFORD COLLECTION, NEW YORK, NEW YORK

STEPHEN HIGGONS, PARIS

THE JOSEPH HIRSHHORN COLLECTION, NEW YORK, NEW YORK

MRS. J. LEE JOHNSON, III, FORT WORTH, TEXAS

MRS. SAMUEL E. JOHNSON, CHICAGO, ILLINOIS

DR. AND MRS. JOHN J. MCDONOUGH, YOUNGSTOWN, OHIO

MRS. PERCY C. MADEIRA, JR., BERWYN, PENNSYLVANIA

MR. AND MRS. PAUL MELLON, UPPERVILLE, VIRGINIA

W. MYRON OWEN, NEW BEDFORD, MASSACHUSETTS

MR. AND MRS. OGDEN PHIPPS, ROSLYN, NEW YORK

MRS. RICHMAN PROSKAUER, NEW YORK, NEW YORK

MRS. EVERETT D. REESE, COLUMBUS, OHIO

MR. AND MRS. LEO M. ROGERS, NEW YORK, NEW YORK

MR. AND MRS. EDGAR SCOTT, VILLANOVA, PENNSYLVANIA

MR. AND MRS. BENJAMIN SONNENBERG, NEW YORK, NEW YORK

MR. AND MRS. A. VARICK STOUT, GREENWICH, CONNECTICUT

LANSING W. THOMS, ST. LOUIS, MISSOURI

MRS. GERTRUDE WHITTEMORE UPSON, MIDDLEBURY, CONNECTICUT

MRS. WILLIAM COXE WRIGHT, ST. DAVIDS, PENNSYLVANIA

ADDISON GALLERY OF AMERICAN ART, PHILLIPS ACADEMY, ANDOVER, MASSACHUSETTS

THE BALTIMORE MUSEUM OF ART, BALTIMORE, MARYLAND

THE PEABODY INSTITUTE, BALTIMORE, MARYLAND

MUSEUM OF FINE ARTS, BOSTON, MASSACHUSETTS

THE ART INSTITUTE OF CHICAGO, CHICAGO, ILLINOIS

CINCINNATI ART MUSEUM, CINCINNATI, OHIO

FLINT INSTITUTE OF ARTS, FLINT, MICHIGAN

GLASGOW ART GALLERY AND MUSEUM, GLASGOW

JOSLYN ART MUSEUM, OMAHA, NEBRASKA

LOS ANGELES COUNTY MUSEUM OF ART, LOS ANGELES, CALIFORNIA

NEW BRITAIN MUSEUM OF AMERICAN ART, NEW BRITAIN, CONNECTICUT

THE NEW YORK PUBLIC LIBRARY, NEW YORK, NEW YORK

THE METROPOLITAN MUSEUM OF ART, NEW YORK, NEW YORK

PHILADELPHIA MUSEUM OF ART, PHILADELPHIA, PENNSYLVANIA

MUSEUM OF ART, RHODE ISLAND SCHOOL OF DESIGN, PROVIDENCE, RHODE ISLAND

MUSEUM OF ART, CARNEGIE INSTITUTE, PITTSBURGH, PENNSYLVANIA

THE CHRYSLER ART MUSEUM, PROVINCETOWN, MASSACHUSETTS

CITY ART MUSEUM OF ST. LOUIS, MISSOURI

THE CORCORAN GALLERY OF ART, WASHINGTON

WORCESTER ART MUSEUM, WORCESTER, MASSACHUSETTS

Introduction

I AM very much disappointed that my compatriots have so little liking for any of my work," Mary Cassatt wrote an American friend regarding a New York exhibition of her paintings in 1895.[1] The attendance was poor and sales very few. Two years earlier a similar exhibition had been held at Durand-Ruel's in Paris. It was her first comprehensive exhibition and she had waited until she was almost fifty years old before making arrangements to hold it. She had worked tirelessly ever since coming to live in Paris in 1874, concentrating on the perfecting of her talents, unhurried in any desire to have her work shown, confident that time would give her her rightful place in the hierarchy of her fellow artists. As a result of this Paris exhibition she won the respect of her Impressionist friends as well as receiving favorable reviews from the majority of the Paris critics and she was satisfied that she had made her mark. In France, she asked for no more than this recognition.

From her own country, however, she expected more. She considered herself an American—although a transplanted one—and hoped that her countrymen would appreciate her work for its native quality. She was emphatic in telling the only biographer who wrote a book about her during her lifetime, "I am American . . . clearly and frankly American."[2] She added that her father's family were of French origin, hav-

ing borne the name Cossart. They left France in 1662 and after a short time in Holland crossed the ocean and settled in the colony of New Amsterdam. Her mother's forefathers came from Scotland to America about 1700. She was born in 1844 in Allegheny City, which later became a part of Pittsburgh. When she was seven, her parents took her, along with her sister and brothers, to Europe where they remained for seven years. The children went to school in France and Germany and learned both languages. Her biographer, Achille Ségard, mentions, however, that Mary Cassatt spoke French with an imperceptible American accent which gave a definite inflection to certain phrases even after she had lived in France for over forty-six years with only three short trips back to her homeland.

Her correspondence with the many members of her family who often came to visit her was an important link with her native country. She always kept her legal residence in Philadelphia, even though her parents and sister Lydia joined her in Paris permanently in 1877.

In the early years of her life abroad, she conscientiously sent her paintings for exhibition to New York and Philadelphia. After her success in her first Impressionist Exhibition (the Fourth) in Paris in 1879, in which she showed *Lydia in a Loge, Wearing a Pearl Necklace* (no. 15), she sent this painting and another portrait to the third exhibition of the Society of American Artists in New York. A few critics praised

[1] In a letter sent to the author by Miss Mathilda Brownell, a New York artist friend of Miss Cassatt.

[2] Achille Ségard, *Mary Cassatt*, Paris, 1913, p. 2.

her work there but most of them tempered their comments with some adverse criticism. These were probably the first Impressionist paintings to be shown in America and they were not understood. They were usually either skied or placed in a dark corner. After a time she ceased to send entries even though as early as 1878 she had written to J. Alden Weir in answer to an invitation to exhibit with the Society, "Your exhibition interests me very much. I wish I could have sent something, I am afraid it is too late now. We expect to have our annual [Impressionist] exhibition here and there are so few of us that we are each required to contribute all we have. You know how hard it is to inaugurate anything like independent action among French artists, and we are carrying on a despairing fight and need all our forces, as every year there are new deserters. I always have a hope that at some future time I shall see New York the artist's ground. I think you will create an American school."[3]

She welcomed many American artists and students to her Paris studio and was always kind and generous to them with her time and interest. She exchanged paintings with Alfred Collins who, together with Walter Gay, came to see her while studying with Bonnat during the 70's. Later Adolphe Borie came, also Carroll Tyson and George Biddle from Philadelphia. Forbes Watson, the critic, wrote, "One couldn't listen to her pouring out her ardor and her understanding, without feeling his conviction in the importance of art to civilization intensified."[4] Many Americans came to visit her on their trips to Europe, keeping her in touch with her native land and bringing her news of other friends and family. These strong ties bound her to America and it is therefore with admirable acumen that André Mellerio, the French critic, wrote of her, "She remains exclusively of her people.... Hers is a direct and significant expression of the American character."[5] In trying to sum up just what this American character is one may say that there is a certain freshness and a directness which is free of affectation. Also there is a dignified reserve in contrast to the usual French "abandon"—a reserve which to the more demonstrative French appears as aloofness. Then, too, there is much vigor and youthful vitality in her work. She fused all these attributes with a deep sympathy for the great, classic painting tradition of France.

How fortunate she was to have arrived in Paris in 1874 to begin her career just as the tremendous artistic innovations of Impressionism were being formulated. She became a part of the struggle to liberate art from the hidebound academic establishment and to gain acceptance for a new way of seeing and thinking. As a self-taught, disciplined, determined young person, indomitable in her pursuit of art, she accepted this challenge as her own. Her ambition had forced her to go to Europe, since in the 1860's there were no art schools in America where she could get the training she wanted. After studying intensively and copying master works in the galleries of Italy, Spain, and the Netherlands, she developed her own style to such a degree that she was able to send paintings to the Paris Salons and have a number of them accepted.

[3] Frederick A. Sweet, *Miss Mary Cassatt: Impressionist from Pennsylvania*, Norman, Oklahoma, 1966, p. 48.

[4] Forbes Watson, *Mary Cassatt*, New York, 1932, p. 12.

[5] André Mellerio, "Mary Cassatt," *L'Art et les Artistes*, vol. XII (Nov. 1910), p. 72.

After settling in Paris, she was persuaded by her family to submit to the usual studio routine under Charles Chaplin, a typical academician. But she was miserable there. Her ideals were already well established and she refused to be subdued by his imitative formulas. This episode, therefore, was as brief as possible and she returned to work in her own studio, where Degas came in 1877 to invite her to join a group who were then called, at his insistence, the "Independents." She accepted his invitation with alacrity. She later told her biographer, "At last I could work with absolute independence without considering the opinion of a jury. I had already recognized who were my true masters. I admired Manet, Courbet, and Degas. I hated conventional art—I began to live."[6]

At once Degas took her under his wing. For the 1879 Impressionist Exhibition he sent in the list of her works together with his own and he proceeded to guide her, not as a pupil, but as a respected ally. He taught her a love of form and an abhorrence of useless detail. They soon found that they shared a reverence for drawing. He encouraged her to pursue drawing on copper which excluded all inexactitude and demanded great discipline. With his encouragement she continued to make prints throughout most of her career. He once complained that he could not do likewise because he had to earn his living. Actually one thing they had in common was the fact that they had sufficient private means not to have to depend entirely on the sale of their art for a living. They were both urban painters, concerned with people rather than landscapes. Degas suggested that she do portraits of people, giving their faces the same expression as that given to their bodies. In an

[6]Achille Ségard, *op. cit.*, p. 8.

important painting, *Little Girl in a Blue Armchair* (no. 11), which demonstrated these precepts, we know that in advising her, Degas actually went so far as to paint one area of the background himself.

Both painters were cooly rational persons, having a sense of detachment as a basic characteristic. Degas once admitted that they had identical intellectual dispositions. However, in temperament they were very different. He was a true cynic with the disenchantment produced by European civilization, whereas she inherited the optimism of a vigorous young country. His biting sarcasm contrasted sharply with her good nature. They both had highly cultivated minds and manners and were aristocratic in bearing. His irony and detached attitude toward humanity were far removed from her sympathetic approach. They were nevertheless close friends, mutually helpful to each other.

One questions to what extent they were true Impressionist painters. Degas always said that he was not an Impressionist. He disliked the term and continued to repudiate it even after it came into general use. After he finished painting his racecourse pictures and some beach scenes of about 1869 he seldom painted outdoors. Mary Cassatt, however, continued plein-air painting throughout her career. They both used bright, prismatic color but unlike the true Impressionists and the Neo-Impressionists, Cassatt used black in her palette. The artists' friend Duranty, who often met with the Impressionist group at the Café Guerbois, has written that Chevreul was then establishing his color wheel. Also the work of Rood on the theory of color was published in France in 1881. The Impressionists, and more surely the Neo-Impressionists, adopted these theories and arranged their palettes according to the chromatic tables furnished by the physicists. Following the theory that light, broken up in a prism, gives off seven colors, they adopted these seven colors on their palettes. Having established their "keyboard" they used it, not according to the colors nature showed them, but according to the law of complements—a true law, but applied too strictly by them. Up to this point Duranty agreed with them but eventually he accused the Impressionists of not knowing how to produce anything in depth. "This comes," he said, "from their denial of black, from the absence of this color in their palettes and," he added, "light and shadow are produced by white and black. Then come the colors with their song to set off the ensemble."[7] He felt that in rejecting this basic principle, the Impressionists were thereby handicapped.

Degas and Cassatt both agreed with Duranty and never avoided the use of black. Cassatt's use of lacquer-like black is found in the 1889 portrait of her mother (no. 42). In this painting, as well as *A Woman in Black at the Opera* (no. 18), the influence of Manet is strong. It was Manet who influenced the Impressionists to think of light as the principal factor in painting. He urged them to paint outdoors, although he did not often practice what he preached. Degas, on the contrary, was always true to his convictions. Being aware of how difficult he was—flying off into rages without warning and being bitingly sarcastic—Cassatt's close friend, Mrs. H. O. Havemeyer, once asked her, "How could you get on with him?" "Oh," she answered, "I am independent! I can live alone and I love to work. Sometimes it made him furious that he could not find a chink in my armor, and there would be months when we just could not see each other, and then something I painted would bring us together again. . . . But, [he was] magnificent! And however dreadful he was, he always lived up to his ideals."[8] And to Cassatt he was a generous teacher and counsellor.

Cassatt's and Degas' use of black may very well have been further stimulated by their study of Japanese prints. It was their friend Felix Bracquemond who first brought these prints to their attention. The Japanese used black as a dominant feature in many of their wood-block prints and line was of primary importance. Asymmetry, foreshortening, and the cutting off of figures by the borders proved fascinating to both of them. Use of the arabesque, flattening of the composition, colorful patterns, and the elimination of all superfluous detail were other attributes they admired. Just as Cassatt had learned the art of painting by analyzing works of the masters, she analyzed the Japanese wood-block prints to learn these new lessons of composition.

In 1890 she and Degas together visited the great exhibition held at the École des Beaux-Arts in which over seven hundred Japanese prints were shown. Miss Cassatt bought a number of them and enjoyed them as decorations in her homes throughout the rest of her life. Most of those she bought were handsome figure prints by Utamaro. She proceeded to translate what she found useful in the Japanese style, not only into her painting but also into her preferred graphic medium—a combination of dry point, soft-ground etching and aquatint. In the summer of 1890 she completed a series of ten

[7] Lairs Emile Edmond Duranty, *La Nouvelle Peinture*, Paris, 1946, p. 17.

[8] Louisine W. Havemeyer, *Sixteen to Sixty, Memoirs of a Collector*, New York, 1961, pp. 244–5.

color prints which are among her most original works. When they were exhibited the following year both Degas and Pissarro were charmed by them. Her draftsmanship is masterly, the viewpoint is from a high level in most of them and form is indicated entirely by line, without shading. About the same time, she painted *The Bath* (no. 49), which is clearly related to the color prints, sharing many of the same style characteristics. The boldly striped gown, the large flat patterned rug and the well drawn pitcher are to be found in both the painting and the finest of the color prints, *Woman Bathing*.

The first evidence of the artist's interest in the Japanese had occurred much earlier than 1890. In 1883 Mrs. Robert Moore Riddle and her daughter visited the Cassatts and brought as a present a handsome Canton tea set. In appreciation the artist asked to paint Mrs. Riddle's portrait (no. 34) with the tea set. She was then reminded of the Japanese prints which had been coming in to Paris for some years. She had studied them whenever she had the opportunity. In consequence, as she painted Mrs. Riddle's portrait she gradually introduced some of what she had learned from those prints. The figure became almost a flattened silhouette and its outlines counted as the dominant element in the design. The face was also treated more two-dimensionally with the blue eyes as accents which reflected the intense blue of the china prominently placed in the foreground. The entire effect was quite different from her earlier work.

From the triumph of this enlargement of her style under the Japanese influence, she progressed to further explorations. One of her good friends, Mrs. Potter Palmer, was placed in charge of arrangements for the Woman's Build-ing at the 1893 World's Columbian Exposition in Chicago. She asked Miss Cassatt to paint a large mural to fill the south tympanum in the main hall of the building. Mrs. Palmer had to defend her choice of this artist who, she said, ". . . is unknown among us." In doing so she stressed the fact that Miss Cassatt had built a vast studio and had the ground excavated with a sunken trench so that the canvas could be lowered into it while she worked on the upper section.[9] The subject given her was "Modern Woman." In describing it one critic wrote, "The central portion of Miss Cassatt's panel shows us a group of young women gathering apples in a pleasant orchard. On the right is a band of ladies variously engaged. One is playing upon a stringed instrument, while another poses in one of the attitudes of the modern skirt-dance. On the left we have Fame, a flying figure, pursued by a flock of ducks and women. The border of the tympanum is very charming; the children quite beautifully painted."[10]

While working at this ambitious project the artist wrote to Mrs. Palmer, "I have been half a dozen times on the point of asking Degas to come and see my work, but if he happens to be in the mood he would demolish me so completely that I could not pick myself up in time to finish for the exhibition. Still, he is the only man I know whose judgment would be a help to me."[11] She strove to make the general effect bright and gay. She said that she reserved all the seriousness for the execution, for the drawing

[9]Aline Saarinen, *The Proud Possessors*, New York, 1958, p. 21.

[10]Maude Howe Elliott, *Art and Handicraft in the Woman's Building of the World's Columbian Exposition*, Chicago, 1893, pp. 31–32.

[11]Julia M. H. Carson, *Mary Cassatt*, New York, 1916, p. 98.

and painting. It was a serious work and a very able one, but at the close of the Exposition it was removed from the hall and is now lost or was destroyed.

Degas evidently knew of her work on the mural and spoke to Pissarro about it who, in turn, wrote to his son Lucien, "Speaking about Miss Cassatt's decoration, I wish you could have heard the conversation I had with Degas on what is known as 'decoration.' I am wholly of his opinion; for him it [a decorative mural] is an ornament that should be made with a view to its place in an ensemble, it requires the collaboration of architect and painter. The decorative picture is an absurdity; a picture complete in itself is not a decoration."[12]

Of course, Degas was right. Handsome as Cassatt's mural probably was, it was placed about forty feet above the floor of the hall so that one had to crane one's neck to see it. We do not know the exact measurements of it, only that at the center it was $12\frac{1}{2}$ feet high. Durand-Ruel saw the central section before it left Paris and was so impressed by it that he offered to buy it at once. The fact that it was done when she had reached her full potential as an artist makes its present loss particularly unfortunate.

After sending the completed mural to Chicago, Cassatt went to Antibes for the winter months and while there painted *The Boating Party* (no. 53). It is the largest of her canvases other than the mural, which may be accounted for by the fact that it followed soon after and she had grown accustomed to a larger format. She mentioned in regard to the mural that her figures were slightly under life-size, although

they seemed as large as life. Much the same is true of *The Boating Party*. The influence of her study of Japanese prints is very apparent in this bold composition. The relationship to Manet's *In the Boat* of 1879 is also to be noted. We know that she admired this painting by Manet and persuaded her friend, Mrs. H. O. Havemeyer, to buy it. But her treatment of the subject is different. The powerful, dark figure of the boatman is offset by the handsome curves of the boat and sail. Thrusting across these is the strong diagonal formed by the oar and the arm of the man, leading the eye to the figures of the mother and child. The delicate patterns found within their silhouettes, including the shadow over the child's face, contrast admirably with the larger compositional lines. This painting, together with *The Bath* (no. 49) and the series of color prints, epitomizes Mary Cassatt's absorption of Japanese methods and her ability to translate them into her own mature style.

From the following year comes another boating picture, *Summertime* (no. 55), which is interesting to compare with *The Boating Party*. One can imagine the artist thinking that after all she was part of the Impressionist group and should not wholly forget its precepts. This picture follows much more closely what the Impressionists were envisioning even to the broken color, sparkling brushwork, and sunny atmosphere. There is nevertheless evidence of the artist's advancing style in the overall pattern, the long line of the boat stopped by the strong spotting of the ducks on the water and the elimination of non-essentials in the painting of the figures and ducks.

In her study of old masters, Mary Cassatt had developed a reverence for the work of Holbein. In the 1890's his influence evidently came to

[12] John D. Kysela, S. J., "Mary Cassatt's Mystery Mural and the World's Fair of 1893," *Art Quarterly*, vol. 29, no. 2 (1966), p. 137.

the fore as she concentrated more on three-dimensional form in rendering heads and bodies, allowing her backgrounds to flatten, sometimes tapering off in an arabesque. In the pastel *In the Garden* (no. 52), the heads are treated as strongly rounded forms whereas flat patterns not only fill the background but also appear on the costumes of the mother and child. This focus of interest on three-dimensional form is even more apparent in *Breakfast in Bed* (no. 58), one of the artist's most intricate compositions. The well rounded arms are rendered by means of short strokes that follow the form closely, brilliantly portraying solid, well-stacked flesh. The varied whites of the pillow and gowns are also notable, enclosed by three flat areas of green. This is one of the most captivating of Cassatt's many mother and child subjects which have placed her in a unique position as the most distinguished painter of this subject. Because she has few peers in this field she is primarily associated with it. Actually she portrayed just as many older children alone and even more young women. She painted the world that she knew, and limited her subjects accordingly. In the 1890's when she was in her prime she devoted a large measure of her interest toward mothers and their babies. Those babies could not be expected to hold a pose and were therefore a special challenge to her draftsmanship, visual memory, and calm perseverance.

In contrast to the more finished paintings and pastels, throughout Cassatt's career we find delightful, spontaneous sketches, some of which relate to her graphic work. In her sketches, as in many of her paintings, she would concentrate on just the head or figure, leaving the surrounding areas lightly and tastefully suggested.

Interior with a French Screen (no. 25) is one such sketch, still in a more Impressionist manner, in which the study of light is most important. *Picking Flowers in a Field* (no. 5), also from the earlier period, is as close to a landscape as can be found in her work. Another quick sketch, *In the Meadow* (no. 22), shows a group of figures seated outdoors on the grass. They are described with broad brush strokes that appear to be entirely spontaneous. The effect is altogether refreshing. *Long Gloves, The Bonnet*, and *Woman Arranging Her Veil* (nos. 40, 41, 43) are closely connected with her series of twelve drypoints exhibited in her 1891 Paris exhibition, together with the ten color prints. In each of these three pastels Cassatt developed the head and arms and let the rest taper off in an arabesque form. The sketch for the Chicago mural (no. 51) is even more freely drawn. It possesses a lack of restraint that is delightful. The *Head of Reine Lefebvre* (no. 67) from as late as 1902, is equally spirited and brisk. In this exhibition, an effort has been made to include many of these sketches and unfinished pictures in order to emphasize the spontaneous and free quality of much of her work.

In 1898 complete concentration on her work was interrupted by her sojourn in America. She remained there for almost six months, visiting her brothers in Philadelphia as well as such friends as the Hammonds and Mrs. Montgomery Sears in Boston, the Whittemores (no. 60) and A. A. Popes in Connecticut, and the Havemeyers and Stillmans in New York. She found that she was able to arouse the interest of quite a number of these friends in the acquisition of paintings. She spent many months traveling with the Havemeyers to help them form their

17

great art collection, now mostly at The Metro-politan Museum of Art. "She was the most devoted friend, the wisest counsellor, the most faithful ally anyone ever had." Mrs. Havemeyer wrote of these excursions, "Without her aid, I should never have been able to make the collection."[13] When she returned to Europe she determined to help not only the Havemeyers but other friends as well in their art purchases. She took her own art more for granted and failed to give it the same complete attention. It suffered in consequence, especially after 1905. Immediately after her return it was not obvious. The portrait of *Mme. Aude and Her Daughters* (no. 62) is as strong as any she ever produced and through the years until 1910 flashes of her full talents asserted themselves, but in almost every case she had to labor to achieve the results. For *Mother and Child in a Boat* (no. 73) of 1908 there are innumerable studies and sketches. The same is true of *Françoise in Green, Sewing* (no. 74), the watercolor in this exhibition (no. 79) being one example. Another example of numerous trials for a satisfactory composition (some better than others) is *Antoinette at Her Dressing Table* (no. 75). The subject, with its typical gesture of the model to smoothe her hair as she looks into a hand mirror, is one entirely within the experience of the artist. It has the calm reserve about it that is evident throughout Cassatt's work—a certain detachment and lack of any impulsive action. The prominent "s"

[13]Louisine W. Havemeyer, *op. cit.*, p. 373.

curve in the composition is interrupted by the small circle of the hand mirror, echoed in that of the larger mirror. The warm and cool colors are also handsomely balanced.

In 1911, Mary Cassatt joined her brother Gardner and his family on a trip to Egypt which ended tragically with her brother's sudden illness and death. As a result, she had a complete breakdown and did no work for almost two years. Also her incipient blindness was pro-gressing rapidly. In 1913, she tried courageously to work again, using the medium of pastels entirely, as Degas did when his eyesight was failing. *The Crochet Lesson* (no. 76) dates from that year—almost her last year of work for she stopped entirely in 1914. As her eyesight dimmed during those last years, her colors became brighter and sometimes are quite strident. However, she thought these works her finest and was delighted to have Mrs. Havemeyer acquire three for her collection.

She lived on through World War I in France, surviving her friend Degas who died in 1917. She stayed mostly in the south at Grasse, since her château at Mesnil-Theribus was in the battle zone. In the ensuing generations many women painters have come to the fore, especially in America, but so far none has surpassed Mary Cassatt.

ADELYN D. BREESKIN
Curator of Contemporary Art
National Collection of Fine Arts
Smithsonian Institution

Catalogue

NOTES TO THE CATALOGUE

BrCR *followed by a number in the catalogue entry refers to the picture's listing in Adelyn Breeskin's* Mary Cassatt: A Catalogue Raisonné of the Oils, Pastels, Watercolors, and Drawings *(Smithsonian Institution Press, Washington, D.C., 1970). The reader may refer to this publication for the complete provenance and exhibition history of each work in this exhibition.*

Dimensions are given in inches, height preceding width.

1
PORTRAIT OF MRS. CURREY; SKETCH OF MR. CASSATT

c. 1871
Oil on canvas, 32 x 27 in.
Unsigned
Lent by W. Myron Owen, New Bedford,
    Massachusetts
BrCR 11

In her youth, Mrs. Currey had worked for the Cassatt family. When Mary came home after studying painting in Paris, she asked Mrs. Currey to pose for her and then gave her the sketch. This canvas also includes a sketch of the artist's father.

2
TOREADOR

1873
Oil on canvas, 32¼ x 25¼ in.
Inscribed at lower left: *M.S.C./Seville/1873*
Lent by The Art Institute of Chicago, Bequest
    of Mrs. Sterling Morton
BrCR 23

In 1872 and 1873, convinced that the best way to learn to paint was to study and copy in the museums of Europe, Mary Cassatt journeyed through Italy, Spain, and the Netherlands. This painting reflects her studies of the Italian and Spanish masters.

3
COPY AFTER FRANS HALS

c. 1873
Oil on canvas, 18¼ x 28½ in.
Unsigned
Lent by Mrs. Percy C. Madeira, Jr., Berwyn,
    Pennsylvania
BrCR 25

This is a copy of Frans Hals' painting in Haarlem entitled *Meeting of the Officers of the Cluveniers-Doelen*, 1633. In later years Mary Cassatt was proud of this copy and would show it to young art students, assuring them that such an exercise was essential to their development.

4
YOUNG WOMAN IN A HAT SEATED ON THE GROUND UNDER TREES

c. 1869
Oil on canvas, 13 x 9½ in.
Inscribed at lower right: *Mary Cassatt*
Lent anonymously
BrCR 7

This is the type of small painting which the artist sent home to be sold by Teubner, the local gilder, framer, and art salesman.

5

PICKING FLOWERS IN A FIELD

c. 1875
Oil on wood, 10½ x 13½ in.
Inscribed at lower right: *Mary Cassatt*
Lent by Mrs. William Coxe Wright, St. Davids,
    Pennsylvania
BrCR 42

This sketch is as close to a landscape as Mary Cassatt ever came. She was much more interested in painting people. However, she posed most of her models outdoors.

6

MRS. DUFFEE SEATED ON A STRIPED SOFA, READING

1876
Oil on wood, 13¾ x 10½ in.
Inscribed at upper left: *M. S. Cassatt / Paris / 1876*
Lent by the Museum of Fine Arts, Boston,
    Massachusetts, Bequest of John T. Spaulding
BrCR 47

This is one of nearly a dozen of Cassatt's early paintings on wood.
Also called *Young Woman Reading*.

7

THE READER

1877
Oil on canvas, 32 x 25½ in.
Inscribed at both lower left and lower right:
    M. S. Cassatt / 1877
Lent anonymously
BrCR 50

Throughout her career Miss Cassatt limited her subjects to what she knew and understood thoroughly. There are many studies such as this, of a young woman reading.
Also called *Femme assise, habillée en blanc*.

8

PORTRAIT OF LYDIA CASSATT, THE ARTIST'S SISTER

1878
Oil on canvas, 30½ x 22¾ in.
Inscribed at lower left: *Mary Cassatt*
Lent by the Joslyn Art Museum, Omaha, Nebraska
BrCR 51

This is one of a number of instances in which the artist executed more than one painting of essentially the same composition. Here the background is simple; in another version it is elaborated by a view through a window.
Also called, in the Cassatt catalogue raisonné, *Lydia Reading the Morning Paper (No. 1)*.

9

PORTRAIT OF MADAME X DRESSED FOR THE MATINEE

1878
Oil on canvas, 39½ x 31¾ in.
Inscribed at lower left: *Mary Cassatt*
Lent anonymously
BrCR 54

"Une Americaine, belle soeur d'un frère de M.C.," wrote one French authority concerning this painting which must be of either Harriet Buchanan, or Miss Carter, both sisters of Miss Cassatt's sisters-in-law.

10

PORTRAIT OF THE ARTIST

1878
Gouache on paper, 23½ x 17½ in.
Inscribed at lower left: *Mary Cassatt*
Lent by Mrs. Richman Proskauer, New York,
    New York
BrCR 55

The informality of this pose reflects Degas' teaching. See no. 77.

11
LITTLE GIRL IN A BLUE ARMCHAIR

1878
Oil on canvas, 35 x 51 in.
Inscribed at lower left: *Mary Cassatt*
Lent from the Collection of Mr. and Mrs. Paul
    Mellon, Upperville, Virginia
BrCR 56

In a letter to the dealer, Ambroise Vollard, the artist wrote around 1900, "Sir, I wanted to return to your place yesterday to talk to you about the portrait of the little girl in the blue armchair. I did it in '78 or '79. It was the portrait of a child of a friend of Mr. Degas. I had done the child in the armchair and he found it good and advised me on the background and he even worked on it. I sent it to the American section of the big exposition '79 [actually 1878]. They refused it. As Mr. Degas had found it to be good, I was furious, all the more so since he had worked on it. At that time this appeared new and the jury consisted of three people of which one was a pharmacist!" (Ambroise Vollard, *Recollections of a Picture Dealer*, Boston, 1936).

Also called *Enfant dans le salon bleu* and, in the Cassatt catalogue raisonné, *The Blue Room*.

12
THE NURSE

1878
Oil on canvas, 28 7/8 x 36 1/4 in.
Inscribed at lower left: *Mary Cassatt*
Lent by Mr. and Mrs. A. Varick Stout, Greenwich,
    Connecticut
BrCR 57

This sketch shows the artist's early interest in such a domestic scene as a nurse in the park with her small charges.

13
IN THE BOX

c. 1879
Oil on canvas, 17 x 24 in.
Unsigned
Lent by Mr. and Mrs. Edgar Scott, Villanova,
    Pennsylvania
BrCR 62

Mrs. Cassatt wrote to her son, Alexander, in November 1883, "Annie [Mrs. Thomas A. Scott], went to Durand-Ruel's the other day and bought a picture by Mary, perhaps you remember it—two young girls at the theatre" (F. A. Sweet, *Miss Mary Cassatt, Impressionist from Philadelphia*, 1966, p. 86).

Also called *Au balcon*.

14
LYDIA LEANING ON HER ARMS, SEATED IN A LOGE

c. 1879
Pastel on paper, 21 5/8 x 17 3/4 in.
Inscribed at lower left: *Mary Cassatt*
Lent anonymously
BrCR 63

The pose resembles that of Degas' portrait of Mary Cassatt (Collection André Meyer, New York, New York) executed at about the same time.

15
LYDIA IN A LOGE, WEARING A PEARL NECKLACE

1879
Oil on canvas, 31 5/8 x 23 in.
Inscribed at lower left: *Mary Cassatt*
Lent by Mrs. William Coxe Wright, St. Davids,
    Pennsylvania
BrCR 64

This is one of the artist's most important paintings and was shown in the Fourth Impressionist

Exhibition of 1879.

Also called *The Sister of the Artist in a Loge; La loge de théâtre; Jeune femme dans une loge; Au théâtre; Dans la loge;* and *Lady in a Loge at the Opera.*

16
WOMAN AND CHILD DRIVING

1879
Oil on canvas, 35 ¼ x 51 ½ in.
Inscribed at lower right: *Mary Cassatt*
Lent by The Commissioners of Fairmount Park,
    W. P. Wilstach Collection, Courtesy of the
    Philadelphia Museum of Art
BrCR 69

This painting shows the strong influence of Degas, especially in the bold cropping of the pony and cart and the asymmetry of the composition. The groom on the jump-seat serves as a splendid foil to the delicately featured child and also lends a humorous note to this vigorous work.

The little girl is Odile Fèvre, a niece of Degas. The woman is the artist's sister, Lydia.

17
PORTRAIT OF AN ITALIAN LADY

c. 1879
Oil on canvas, 31 ⅝ x 24 ⅜ in.
Inscribed at lower left: *M. S. Cassatt*
Lent anonymously
BrCR 938

This may represent Mme. Marie Del Sarte, who ran a fashionable boarding school for young ladies in Paris. Louisine Waldron Elder, later Mrs. H. O. Havemeyer, and Mary Ellison of Philadelphia, both friends of the artist, attended the school.

18
A WOMAN IN BLACK AT THE OPERA

1880
Oil on canvass, 32 x 26 in.

Inscribed at lower left: *Mary Cassatt*
Lent by the Museum of Fine Arts, Boston,
    Massachusetts, Charles Henry Hayden Fund
BrCR 73

The Museum of Fine Arts astutely bought this fine painting as early as 1910 and another, equally fine, *Five O'Clock Tea,* a few years later.

Also called *La loge à l'opéra; Dans la loge;* and *At the Opera.*

19
FIVE O'CLOCK TEA

1880
Oil on canvas, 25 ½ x 36 ½ in.
Inscribed at lower left: *Mary Cassatt*
Lent by the Museum of Fine Arts, Boston,
    Massachusetts, Maria Hopkins Fund
BrCR 78

The tea service, which is still in the Cassatt family, was made for Miss Cassatt's grandmother Mary Stevenson, after whom the artist was named. Lydia Cassatt appears at the left. The painting was included in both the Fifth and Sixth Impressionist Exhibitions of 1880 and 1881.

Also called *Le thé; Five O'clock;* and *La tasse de thé.*

20
WOMAN BY A WINDOW
FEEDING HER DOG

c. 1880
Oil, gouache, and pastel on canvas, 24 x 16 in.
Inscribed at lower right: *Mary Cassatt*
Lent anonymously
BrCR 84

The combination of media is unusual for Cassatt, a technique she learned from Degas.

Also called *Femme assise jouant avec un chien devant une fenêtre.*

21

MOTHER ABOUT TO WASH HER SLEEPY CHILD

1880
Oil on canvas, 39½ x 25¾ in.
Inscribed at lower left: *Mary Cassatt / 1880*
Lent by the Los Angeles County Museum of Art,
    Bequest of Mrs. Fred Hathaway Bixby
BrCR 90

This is often considered Mary Cassatt's first painting of the mother and child theme. It was shown at the Fifth Impressionist Exhibition, Paris, 1880.

Also called *The Bath* and *La toilette de l'enfant*.

22

IN THE MEADOW (No. 2)

1880
Oil on canvas, 21⅜ x 25⅝ in.
Inscribed at lower right: *Mary Cassatt*
Lent by Mr. and Mrs. B. E. Bensinger, Chicago,
    Illinois
BrCR 93

Also called *Dans la prairie*.

23

LYDIA CROCHETING IN THE GARDEN AT MARLY

1880
Oil on canvas, 26 x 37 in.
Inscribed at lower left: *Mary Cassatt*
Lent by Mrs. Gardner Cassatt, Villanova,
    Pennsylvania
BrCR 98

Degas wrote to his friend, Henri Rouart, "The Cassatts have come back from Marly.... What she did in the country looks very well in studio light. It is much stronger and nobler than what she had last year" (*Degas Letters*, Oxford, 1948, p. 63). It was included in the Sixth Impressionist Exhibition, Paris, 1881.

Also called *En brodant* and *Lydia Knitting in the Garden at Marly*.

24

LYDIA SEATED ON A PORCH, CROCHETING

1881
Gouache on canvas, 15 x 24 in.
Inscribed at lower left: *Mary Cassatt*
Lent by Mr. Lansing W. Thoms, St. Louis,
    Missouri
BrCR 102

Also called *Woman on Park Bench* and *La Serre*.

25

INTERIOR WITH A FRENCH SCREEN

c. 1881
Oil on canvas, 17 x 22½ in.
Inscribed at lower right: *Mary Cassatt*
Lent by Mrs. Percy C. Madeira, Jr., Berwyn,
    Pennsylvania
BrCR 114

26

LYDIA WORKING AT A TAPESTRY FRAME

c. 1881
Oil on canvas, 25¾ x 36¼ in.
Inscribed at lower right: *Mary Cassatt*
Lent by the Flint Institute of Arts, Flint, Michigan
BrCR 115

This was the last picture for which Lydia Cassatt posed. She died November 7, 1882.

27

MASTER ROBERT KELSO CASSATT

c. 1882
Oil on canvas, 19 x 22¾ in.

Unsigned
Lent by Alexander J. Cassatt, Cecilton, Maryland
BrCR 119

Young Robert, second son of Alexander J. Cassatt, was the artist's favorite nephew. She hoped for a time that he would become an artist and sometimes would take him along on sketching trips.

28
THE LOGE

1882
Oil on canvas, 31½ x 25¼ in.
Inscribed at lower right: *Mary Cassatt*
National Gallery of Art, Chester Dale Collection
BrCR 121

The blonde young lady has been said to be Geneviève Mallarmé, the daughter of Miss Cassatt's friend, Stéphane Mallarmé, the poet. The brunette is Miss Mary Ellison, a Philadelphia friend of the artist.

Also called *The Opera Box* and, in the Cassatt catalogue raisonné, *Two Young Ladies in a Loge.*

29
SUSAN ON A BALCONY
HOLDING A DOG

1883
Oil on canvas, 39½ x 25½ in.
Inscribed at lower right: *Mary Cassatt*
Lent by The Corcoran Gallery of Art,
    Washington, D.C.
BrCR 125

Miss Cassatt always had pet dogs, mostly toy griffons. The one seen here was named "Battie." In 1898 when she returned to Philadelphia for a visit, the local newspapers wrote only that she had been studying painting in France and owned the smallest Pekingese dog in the world.

Susan was a cousin of Mathilde Vallet, Cassatt's

housekeeper-maid. This painting was purchased from the artist in 1909 by The Corcoran Gallery.

Also called *Woman with a Dog* and *La femme au chien.*

30
PORTRAIT OF
ALEXANDER J. CASSATT

1883
Oil on canvas, 25½ x 35¾ in.
Unsigned
Lent by Alexander J. Cassatt, Cecilton, Maryland
BrCR 126

Alexander, known to the family as Aleck, was Miss Cassatt's older brother. He later became president of the Pennsylvania Railroad.

31
READING "LE FIGARO"

1883
Oil on canvas, 41 x 33 in.
Inscribed at lower right: *Mary Cassatt*
Lent anonymously
BrCR 128

It is interesting to compare this portrait of the artist's mother with a later one done in 1889.
    See no. 42.

32
YOUNG WOMAN IN BLACK

1883
Oil on canvas, 31½ x 25¼ in.
Inscribed at lower right: *Mary Cassatt*
Lent by The Peabody Institute, Baltimore, Mary-
    land, courtesy of The Baltimore Museum of Art
BrCR 129

The figure shows the influence of Manet, whereas the treatment of the upholstered armchair and the background reflects that of Degas.

33

TWO CHILDREN AT THE SEASHORE

1884
Oil on canvas, 38½ x 29¼ in.
Inscribed at lower right: *Mary Cassatt*
National Gallery of Art, Ailsa Mellon Bruce
   Collection
BrCR 131

In January 1884 Mrs. Cassatt was ill and Mary took her to Spain for her health. It is possible that this painting was executed while they were there.

Also called *Enfants jouant sur la plage; Enfants au bord de la mer; Marine;* and *Children Playing on the Beach.*

34

LADY AT THE TEA TABLE

1883–1885
Oil on canvas, 29 x 24 in.
Inscribed at lower left: *Mary Cassatt / 1885*
Lent by The Metropolitan Museum of Art,
   New York, Gift of the artist, 1923
BrCR 139

This is a portrait of Mrs. Robert Moore Riddle (Mary Johnston Dickinson), a first cousin of Mrs. Robert S. Cassatt, the artist's mother. It was begun in 1883 and finished two years later. Mrs. Cassatt wrote to her son Aleck in 1883, "As they are not very artistic in their likes and dislikes of pictures and as a likeness is a hard thing to make to please the nearest friends, I don't know what the results will be. Annie [Mrs. Riddle's daughter, Mrs. Thomas A. Scott] ought to like it in one respect for both Degas and Raffaëlli said it was 'La distinction même' and Annie goes in for that kind of thing" (F. A. Sweet, *Miss Mary Cassatt, Impressionist from Pennsylvania,* 1966, p. 86).

The Riddle family was not pleased with the portrait, which disappointed Mary Cassatt terribly. She put it away in a closet until Mrs. Havemeyer found it years later and insisted on its being exhibited, in 1914, at Durand-Ruel's, Paris.

35

THE LITTLE SISTERS

c. 1885
Oil on canvas, 18¼ x 21⅞ in.
Inscribed at lower right: *Mary Cassatt*
Lent by the Glasgow Art Gallery and Museum,
   Glasgow
BrCR 142

36

CHILD IN A STRAW HAT

c. 1886
Oil on canvas, 25½ x 19¼ in.
Inscribed at lower right: *Mary Cassatt*
Lent from the Collection of Mr. and Mrs. Paul
   Mellon, Upperville, Virginia
BrCR 143

Also called, in the Breeskin catalogue raisonné, *Little Girl in a Big Straw Hat and a Pinafore.*

37

THE FAMILY

c. 1886
Oil on canvas, 32¼ x 26⅛ in.
Inscribed at lower right: *Mary Cassatt*
Lent by The Chrysler Art Museum,
   Provincetown, Massachusetts
BrCR 145

There is a definite relation between the woman and the little girl in this painting and two of the main figures in the Chicago mural of six years later.

Also called *La Famille; Family Group;* and *Maternité.*

See nos. 48, 51, 82.

38

GIRL ARRANGING HER HAIR

1886
Oil on canvas, 29½ x 24½ in.

Unsigned
National Gallery of Art, Chester Dale Collection
BrCR 146

This painting was executed by Cassatt in order to prove to Degas that she knew the meaning of style. Shown at the Eighth Impressionist Exhibition in 1886, Degas was sufficiently impressed with the painting to acquire it for his personal collection, where it remained until his death.

Also called *Fillette se coiffant; La fille à sa toilette; The Morning Toilet;* and *La toilette.*

39
BABY IN DARK BLUE SUIT, LOOKING OVER HIS MOTHER'S SHOULDER

1889
Oil on canvas, 29 x 23½ in.
Inscribed at lower right: *Mary Cassatt*
Lent by the Cincinnati Art Museum, Cincinnati, Ohio
BrCR 153

Also called *Enfant en costume bleu et jeune femme; Bébé en costume bleu, dans les bras d'une jeune femme;* and *Mother and Child.*

40
THE LONG GLOVES

1889
Pastel on paper, 25½ x 21 in.
Inscribed at lower right: *Mary Cassatt*
Lent by Mrs. Percy C. Madeira, Jr., Berwyn, Pennsylvania
BrCR 157

41
THE BONNET

c. 1889
Oil on canvas, 16¼ x 9¾ in.
Unsigned

26

Lent anonymously
BrCR 160

Related to the drypoint of the same title. Also called *Woman's Head* and *Woman Wearing a Bonnet.*

42
PORTRAIT OF MRS. ROBERT S. CASSATT

c. 1889
Oil on canvas, 38 x 27 in.
Unsigned
Lent by Mrs. Gardner Cassatt, Villanova, Pennsylvania
BrCR 162

This last portrait of the artist's mother is a most incisive statement of the dignity of old age.
See no. 31.

43
WOMAN ARRANGING HER VEIL

c. 1890
Pastel on paper, 25½ x 21½ in.
Inscribed at lower right: *Mary Cassatt*
Lent by the Philadelphia Museum of Art
BrCR 174

Also called *The Black Hat.*

44
MADAME H. DE FLEURY AND HER CHILD

1890
Oil on canvas, 29 x 23½ in.
Inscribed at lower right: *Mary Cassatt*
Lent by Mr. and Mrs. Ogden Phipps, Roslyn, New York
BrCR 175

Mme. de Fleury was a friend of the artist and of Degas.

45
THE BLACK HAT

c. 1890
Pastel on paper, 24 x 18 in.
Unsigned
Lent from the Collection of Mr. and Mrs. Paul
    Mellon, Upperville, Virginia
BrCR 177

Also called *Buste de jeune fille, chapeau noir*
and, in the Cassatt catalogue raisonné, *Portrait of a
Young Girl in a Black, Plumed Hat.*

46
MATERNITY, WITH BABY
OBSERVING SPECTATOR

c. 1890
Pastel on paper, 23 ¾ x 18 in.
Inscribed at upper left: *Mary Cassatt*
Lent by H. Wendell Cherry, Louisville, Kentucky
BrCR 180

The artist's complete understanding of infant
psychology is evident in this splendid study of a
baby looking at the world from the protection of
its mother's or nurse's arms.

47
BABY'S FIRST CARESS

1891
Pastel on paper, 30 x 24 in.
Inscribed at upper left: *Mary Cassatt*
Lent by the New Britain Museum of American
    Art, New Britain, Connecticut, Harriet Russell
    Stanley Fund
BrCR 189

Also called *La caresse.*

48
YOUNG WOMEN PICKING FRUIT

1891
Oil on canvas, 52 x 36 in.

Inscribed at lower right: *Mary Cassatt*
Lent by the Museum of Art, Carnegie Institute,
    Pittsburgh, Pennsylvania
BrCR 197

Cassatt was always keenly interested in clothes,
an interest she shared with Degas. She often bought
gowns from Worth and other fashionable
couturiers to be worn by her models. This canvas
was painted at Bachivillers.
See nos. 37, 51.

49
THE BATH

1892
Oil on canvas, 39 ½ x 26 in.
Inscribed at lower left: *Mary Cassatt*
Lent by The Art Institute of Chicago, Robert A.
    Waller Fund
BrCR 205

The unusual perspective and the partial depic-
tion of objects reflect the influence of Japanese
prints and of photography.
Also called *La toilette* and *La toilette de l'enfant.*

50
THE SAILOR BOY:
GARDNER CASSATT

1892
Pastel on paper, 28 x 23 in.
Inscribed at lower left: *Mary Cassatt / Paris 1892*
Lent by Mrs. Gardner Cassatt, Villanova,
    Pennsylvania
BrCR 208

The boy was the son of the artist's younger
brother, Gardner

51
SKETCH OF YOUNG WOMAN
PICKING FRUIT

1892
Oil on canvas, 23 ½ x 28 ¾ in.

Unsigned
Lent by Stephen Higgons, Paris
BrCR 212

This is a sketch for the full-length figure in the central section of the mural, entitled "Modern Woman," that Miss Cassatt did for the Woman's Building of the World's Columbian Exposition held at Chicago in 1893.

The oil painting *Young Women Picking Fruit* is also related to this mural. At the end of the Exposition, the mural was removed and since was either lost or destroyed.

See nos. 37, 48.

52
IN THE GARDEN

1893
Pastel on paper, 28¾ x 23⅝ in.
Inscribed at lower right: *Mary Cassatt*
Lent by The Baltimore Museum of Art, Cone
    Collection
BrCR 221

53
THE BOATING PARTY

1893
Oil on canvas, 35½ x 46⅛ in.
Unsigned
National Gallery of Art, Chester Dale Collection
BrCR 230

In 1914 Cassatt wrote to Durand-Ruel from Grasse: "About the painting, *La Barque*, I do not want to sell it; I have already promised it to my family. It was done at Antibes 20 years ago—the year my niece came into the world."

Also called *La partie en bateau; La barque; Les canotiers;* and *En canot.*

54
IN THE PARK

c. 1894
Oil on canvas, 29½ x 37½ in.

Inscribed at lower right: *Mary Cassatt*
Lent anonymously
BrCR 239

Although Miss Cassatt is best known for her portrayal of mother and child, here the young woman is definitely a nurse.

55
SUMMERTIME

1894
Oil on canvas, 29 x 38 in.
Inscribed at lower right: *Mary Cassatt*
Lent by the Huntington Hartford Collection,
    New York
BrCR 240

This painting is related to the color print, *Feeding the Ducks.*

56
MADAME AND HER MAID

c. 1894
Pastel on paper, 20 x 29 in.

Inscribed at lower right: *Mary Cassatt*
Lent by Mrs. Florence Gould, Cannes, France
BrCR 241

The fact that Miss Cassatt's companion-maid, Mathilde Vallet, filled such an important place in her life probably influenced her in painting this contrasting character study of two other women.

57
ELLEN MARY CASSATT
IN A WHITE COAT

c. 1896
Oil on canvas, 32 x 23⅝ in.
Inscribed at lower left: *Mary Cassatt*
Lent by Charles W. Hare, Cambridge,
    Massachusetts
BrCR 258

Ellen Mary was the daughter of Gardner
Cassatt, the artist's younger brother.
Also called *The Little Infanta*.

58
BREAKFAST IN BED

1897
Oil on canvas, 25 ⅝ x 29 in.
Inscribed at lower left: *Mary Cassatt*
Lent by Dr. and Mrs. John J. McDonough,
    Youngstown, Ohio
BrCR 275

59
STUDY OF
MRS. CLEMENT B. NEWBOLD

1898
Oil on canvas, 24 x 21 in.
Unsigned
Lent by Mrs. Donald B. Barrows, Bryn Mawr,
    Pennsylvania
BrCR 288

The first portrait of Mrs. Newbold did not
please her parents and they asked Miss Cassatt to
try again. This is the carefully planned sketch for
the second portrait.

60
PORTRAIT OF A GRAND LADY (MRS.
JOHN HOWARD WHITTEMORE)

1898
Pastel on paper, 28 x 23 in.
Inscribed at lower left: *Mary Cassatt*
Lent by Mrs. Gertrude Whittemore Upson,
    Middlebury, Connecticut
BrCR 297

The portrait was painted during Mary Cassatt's
first visit to her native country in a quarter of a
century. She returned to Paris after six months.

61
GARDNER AND ELLEN MARY
CASSATT

1899
Pastel on paper, 25 x 18 ¾ in.
Inscribed at lower right: *Mary Cassatt*
Lent by Mrs. Gardner Cassatt, Villanova,
    Pennsylvania
BrCR 302

This portrait of the artist's nephew and niece
was done during her visit to America in 1898–1899.

62
PORTRAIT OF MME. A. F. AUDE
AND HER TWO DAUGHTERS

1899
Pastel on paper, 21 ⅜ x 31 ⅞
Lent by Collection Durand-Ruel, Paris
BrCR 307

Mme. Aude was the daughter of Paul Durand-
Ruel, Cassatt's and Degas' dealer. Mme. Aude's
older daughter, Madeleine on the left, became the
Comtesse de Brecey; the younger, Thérèse, the
Vicomtesse de Montfort.

63
BABY GETTING UP FROM HIS NAP

1901
Oil on canvas, 36 ⅛ x 29 in.
Inscribed at lower left of tray: *Mary Cassatt*
Lent by The Metropolitan Museum of Art, New
    York, George A. Hearn Fund, 1909
BrCR 342

Cassatt rarely painted still-life, but she sometimes incorporated it as an important element of
her figure paintings.
Also called *Le lever de bébé; Morning Bath;* and
Baby Arises.

64
FAMILY GROUP READING

1901
Oil on canvas, 22 x 44 in.
Inscribed at lower left: *Mary Cassatt*
Lent by the Philadelphia Museum of Art
BrCR 343

Also called *Le livre d'images; Il libro illustrato;* and, in the Cassatt catalogue raisonné, *The Garden Lecture.*

65
MOTHER AND DAUGHTER, BOTH WEARING LARGE HATS

1901
Oil on canvas, 31 ⅞ x 25 ⅝ in.
Inscribed at lower right: *Mary Cassatt*
Lent by Mrs. J. Lee Johnson, III, Fort Worth, Texas
BrCR 345

This is another example of the artist's keen interest in women's fashions.
Also called *Fillette au grand chapeau.*
See no. 48.

66
TWO WOMEN READING

1901
Oil on canvas, 15 x 19 ¼ in.
Inscribed at lower left: *Mary Cassatt*
Lent by Mr. and Mrs. William H. Green, River
    Forest, Illinois
BrCR 346

As with most of the artist's figure studies, this one was painted outdoors.
Also called *La lecture* and *Reading.*

67
SKETCH OF HEAD OF REINE LEFEBVRE

c. 1902
Oil on canvas, 16 x 13 in.

Inscribed at lower right: *M.C.*
Lent anonymously
BrCR 395

This very free sketch of a model's head was done in preparation for the painting of *Reine Lefebvre Holding a Nude Baby.*

68
REINE LEFEBVRE HOLDING A NUDE BABY

1902
Oil on canvas, 26 ⅞ x 22 ⅝ in.
Inscribed at lower right: *Mary Cassatt*
Lent by the Worcester Art Museum, Worcester,
    Massachusetts
BrCR 406

Mary Cassatt preferred using as models for her mothers the young country women who lived near her château at Mesnil-Theribus, Oise. She found that they knew much better how to hold a baby than a professional model; the woman here was only about seventeen years old.

69
YOUNG MOTHER SEWING

1902
Oil on canvas, 36 ⅜ x 29 in.
Inscribed at lower right: *Mary Cassatt*
Lent by The Metropolitan Museum of Art, New
    York, Bequest of Mrs. H. O. Havemeyer, 1929.
    The H. O. Havemeyer Collection.
BrCR 415

70
REINE LEFEBVRE AND MARGOT

c. 1902
Pastel on paper, 31 ¾ x 25 ¾ in.
Inscribed at lower left: *Mary Cassatt*
Lent by Dr. Armand Hammer, Los Angeles,
    California
BrCR 430

71

SIMONE IN A WHITE BONNET
SEATED WITH CLASPED HANDS
(No. 2)

c. 1903
Pastel on paper, 25½ x 16½ in.
Inscribed at lower right: *M.C.*
Lent by Mr. and Mrs. Dale H. Dorn, San Antonio,
Texas
BrCR 440

This is one of many pastels of this blonde model, whom the artist found in the neighborhood of her château in the Oise country.

72

SIMONE TALKING TO HER MOTHER

c. 1904
Oil on canvas, 31⅞ x 25⅝
Inscribed at lower right: *Mary Cassatt*
Lent anonymously
BrCR 451

73

MOTHER AND CHILD IN A BOAT

1908
Oil on canvas, 45½ x 31¾ in.
Inscribed at lower right: *Mary Cassatt*
Lent by the Addison Gallery of American Art,
Phillips Academy, Andover, Massachusetts
BrCR 524

Among Mary Cassatt's later paintings this one occupied much of her attention. There are numerous preparatory sketches for it in oil, pastel, and watercolor.
Also called *Dans la barque.*

74

FRANÇOISE IN GREEN, SEWING

1908
Oil on canvas, 32 x 25½ in.
Inscribed at lower right: *Mary Cassatt*

Lent by the City Art Museum of St. Louis,
Missouri
BrCR 538

Of this model there are over a dozen paintings, pastels, and watercolors.
Also called *Young Girl Threading a Needle* and *Jeune fille brodant.*
See no. 79.

75

ANTOINETTE AT HER
DRESSING TABLE

1909
Oil on canvas, 36½ x 28½ in.
Inscribed at lower right: *Mary Cassatt*
Lent by Mrs. Samuel E. Johnson, Chicago, Illinois
BrCR 543

Both Cassatt and Degas were fascinated by the mirror image. Throughout her career she used mirror reflections to extend space.
Also called *Femme à sa toilette; At the Dressing Table;* and *Jeune femme se mirant auprès de sa table de toilette.*

76

THE CROCHET LESSON

1913
Pastel on paper, 30⅛ x 25½ in.
Inscribed at lower left: *Mary Cassatt*
Lent by the Melvin Gelman Collection,
Washington
BrCR 595

As Mary Cassatt's eyesight failed the colors in her paintings became increasingly intense.
Also called *Jeune fille en corsage bleu et fillette en robe rouge.*

77

SELF-PORTRAIT

c. 1880
Watercolor on paper, 13 x 9½ in.

Inscribed at lower center: *M.C.*
Lent by Mr. A. P. Bersohn, New York, New York
BrCR 618

This quick watercolor sketch appears to be a
better likeness of the artist than the more studied
gouache done two years earlier.
See no. 10.

78
SKETCH OF VERNON LEE
WEARING PINCE-NEZ

1895
Watercolor on paper, 9½ x 6¾ in.
Inscribed at lower right: *Mary Cassatt*
Lent by Mr. and Mrs. Benjamin Sonnenberg,
    New York
BrCR 625

The English writer, Violet Padgett, known as
Vernon Lee, visited Mary Cassatt at Mesnil-
Theribus in July 1895 and then wrote to a friend,
"I liked immensely being at Mesnil. . . . Miss Cassatt
is very nice, simple, an odd mixture of a self-
recognizing artist, with passionate appreciation
in literature, and the almost childish garrulous
American provincial" (F. A. Sweet, *Miss Mary
Cassatt, Impressionist from Pennsylvania*, 1966,
pp. 143–144).

79
FRANÇOISE SEWING (No. 1)

1908
Watercolor on paper, 15¾ x 11⅜ in.
Inscribed at lower right: *M.C.*
Lent by The Joseph H. Hirshhorn Collection,
    New York
BrCR 659

This watercolor is a study for the oil, *Françoise
in Green, Sewing.*
Also called *La petite fille en bleu.*
See no. 74.

80
LITTLE GIRL HOLDING A DOLL

c. 1876
Black crayon on paper, 12 x 9 in.
Inscribed at lower right: *Mary Cassatt*
Lent by Prof. Dorothy Brown, Malibu, California
BrCR 705

81
STUDY FOR
"INTERIOR: ON THE SOFA"

c. 1883
Pencil on paper, 5⅝ x 8⅝ in.
Inscribed at upper right: *M.C.*
Lent by Mrs. Samuel E. Johnson, Chicago, Illinois
BrCR 769

The bold asymmetry of this drawing, the use of
a large area of pattern, and the cropping of the
composition all show the strong influence of Degas'
teaching.
This is a preparatory drawing for the print of
the same title.

82
BABY OF "THE FAMILY" LOOKING
DOWN TO LEFT

c. 1886
Pencil and crayon on paper, 14⅜ x 12¼ in.
Inscribed at upper right:
    To Mr. Keppel / Mary Cassatt
Lent by Gordon K. Allison, New York
BrCR 777

Cassatt copied Holbein at the Louvre and was
especially attracted to Hals, Velázquez and the
Venetians, whose works she also copied. In this
case, the drawing shows the influence of her study
of Holbein.
This is a preparatory study for the painting,
The Family, now in the Chrysler collection.
See no. 37.

83

MOTHER PULLING ON BABY'S STOCKING

c. 1890
Pencil on paper, 10½ x 7⅞ in.
Inscribed at lower right: *Mary Cassatt*
Lent by the Museum of Art, Rhode Island School
    of Design, Gift of Mrs. Gustav Radeke
BrCR 790

This Cassatt drawing is similar to a pastel of the same subject as well as to one of her drypoint prints. In a note on one impression of the drypoint, Miss Cassatt mentions that her parrot was on a perch nearby and the baby's attention was attracted to it.

84

THE FIRST CARESS

1891
Crayon on paper, 10½ x 7½ in.
Inscribed at upper left: *Mr. Avery with / the
    compliments of / Mary Cassatt / Jany, '91, Paris*
Lent by The New York Public Library, Astor,
    Lenox and Tilden Foundations, S. P. Avery
    Collection
BrCR 800

Mr. Samuel P. Avery also owned a large collection of Cassatt's drypoints and color prints, which he left to The New York Public Library.

85

STUDY FOR "IN THE OMNIBUS"

c. 1891
Crayon and pencil on paper, 14⅜ x 10⅝ in.
Inscribed at lower right: *Mary Cassatt*
National Gallery of Art, Rosenwald Collection
BrCR 804

This is the working drawing for the color print of the same title. The man's figure at the right was not used in the print.

86

STUDY FOR "THE COIFFURE" (No. 3)

c. 1891
Pencil on paper, 5⅞ x 4⅜ in.
Inscribed at lower left: *M.C.*
National Gallery of Art, Rosenwald Collection
BrCR 815

A preparatory drawing for the color print of the same title.

87

STUDY FOR "GATHERING FRUIT"

1893
Pastel and charcoal on paper, 11¼ x 10 in.
Unsigned
Lent by Mrs. Lester Avnet, New York
BrCR 821

A preparatory drawing for the color print of the same title (also called *L'Espalier*). The theme of the print is here established, but the lower third of the composition is lacking.

88

TWO LITTLE GIRLS

c. 1897
Pencil on paper, 7½ x 6½ in.
Inscribed at lower right: *à Mlle Mayer /
    compliments de / M. Cassatt*
Lent by Prof. Dorothy Brown, Malibu, California
BrCR 834

89

PORTRAIT SKETCH OF MADAME FONTVEILLE (No. 2)

1902
Pencil on paper, 16 x 11¼ in.
Inscribed at lower right: *Mary Cassatt;* and at
upper right: *Mme Ley Fontveille / Ave. d'Eylau
26*

Lent by Mr. and Mrs. Leo M. Rogers, New York,
New York
BrCR 857

Madame Fontveille was a spiritualist to whom
Mary Cassatt went in 1902 with her friend,
Theodate Pope, for several séances.

90
PORTRAIT OF HERBERT JACOBY

c. 1905
Pencil and watercolor on rice paper, 8 x 10 in.
Inscribed at lower right: *Mary Cassatt*
Lent by Mrs. Everett D. Reese, Columbus, Ohio
BrCR 914

I PORTRAIT OF MRS. CURREY; SKETCH OF MR. CASSATT

2 TOREADOR

3   COPY AFTER FRANS HALS

6 MRS. DUFFEE SEATED ON A STRIPED SOFA, READING

4　YOUNG WOMAN IN A HAT
　　SEATED ON THE GROUND UNDER TREES

5   PICKING FLOWERS IN A FIELD

20   WOMAN BY A WINDOW FEEDING HER DOG

7 THE READER

9　PORTRAIT OF MADAME X DRESSED FOR THE MATINÉE

10 PORTRAIT OF THE ARTIST

II   LITTLE GIRL IN A BLUE ARMCHAIR

13   IN THE BOX

14 LYDIA LEANING ON HER ARMS, SEATED IN A LOGE

16   WOMAN AND CHILD DRIVING

18   A WOMAN IN BLACK AT THE OPERA

21   MOTHER ABOUT TO WASH HER SLEEPY CHILD

23　LYDIA CROCHETING IN THE GARDEN AT MARLY

25   INTERIOR WITH A FRENCH SCREEN

27   MASTER ROBERT KELSO CASSATT

29   SUSAN ON A BALCONY HOLDING A DOG

30   PORTRAIT OF ALEXANDER J. CASSATT

32   YOUNG WOMAN IN BLACK

36   CHILD IN A STRAW HAT

39   BABY IN DARK BLUE SUIT, LOOKING OVER HIS MOTHER'S SHOULDER

33   TWO CHILDREN AT THE SEASHORE

37   THE FAMILY

40　THE LONG GLOVES

42 PORTRAIT OF MRS. ROBERT S. CASSATT

44   MADAME H. DE FLEURY AND HER CHILD

45   THE BLACK HAT

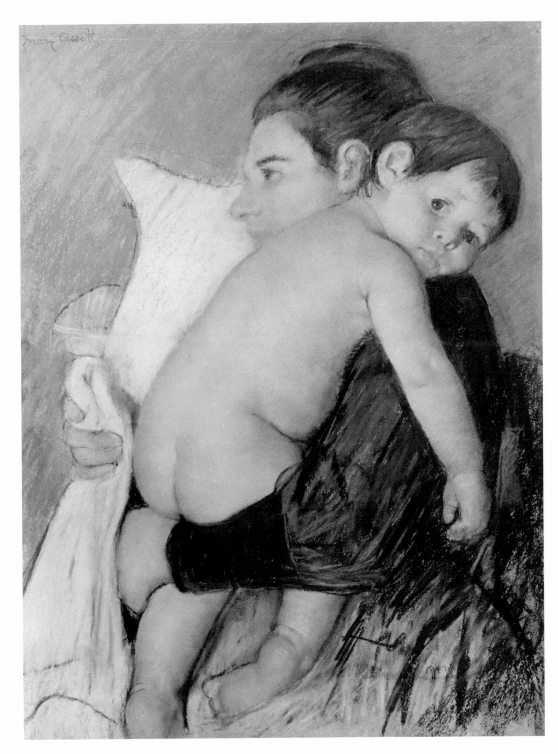

46   MATERNITY, WITH BABY OBSERVING SPECTATOR

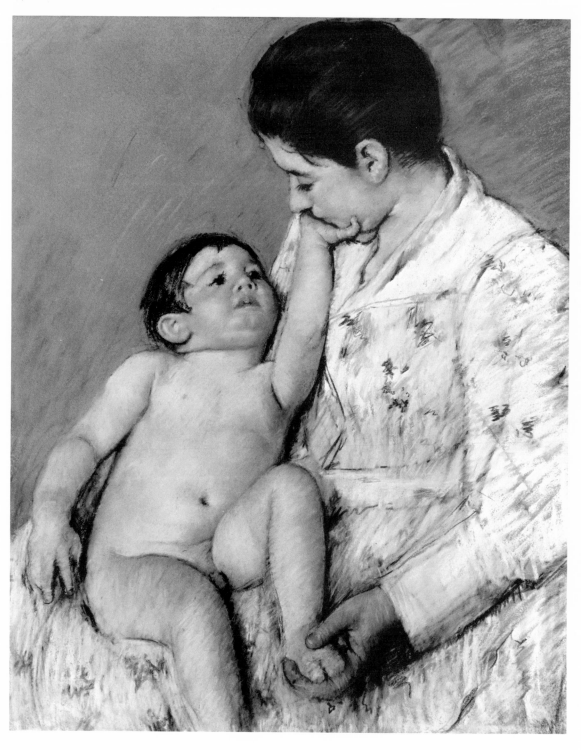

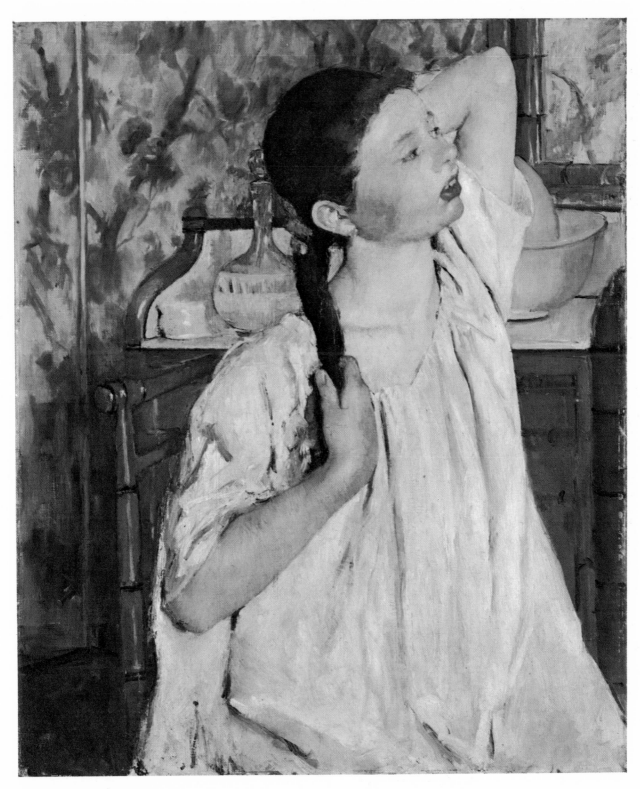

38   GIRL ARRANGING HER HAIR

52   IN THE GARDEN

48   YOUNG WOMEN PICKING FRUIT

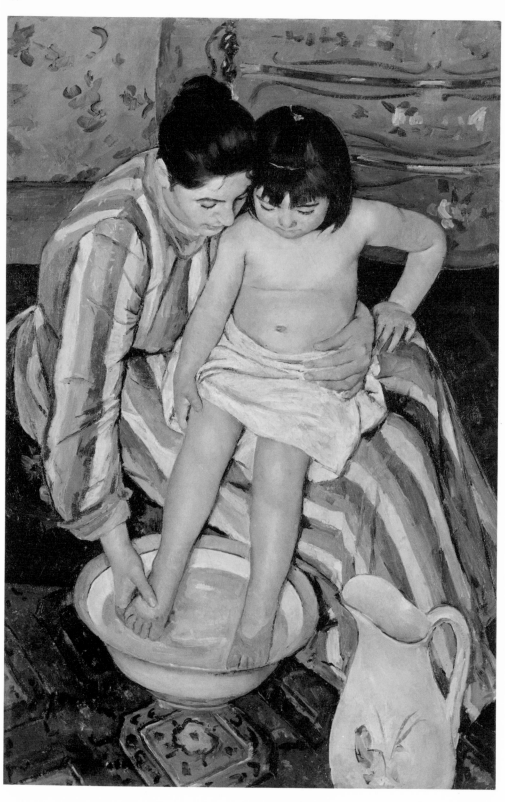

50   THE SAILOR BOY: GARDNER CASSATT

51 SKETCH OF YOUNG WOMAN PICKING FRUIT

56   MADAME AND HER MAID

57 ELLEN MARY CASSATT IN A WHITE COAT

59 STUDY OF MRS. CLEMENT B. NEWBOLD

61   GARDNER AND ELLEN MARY CASSATT

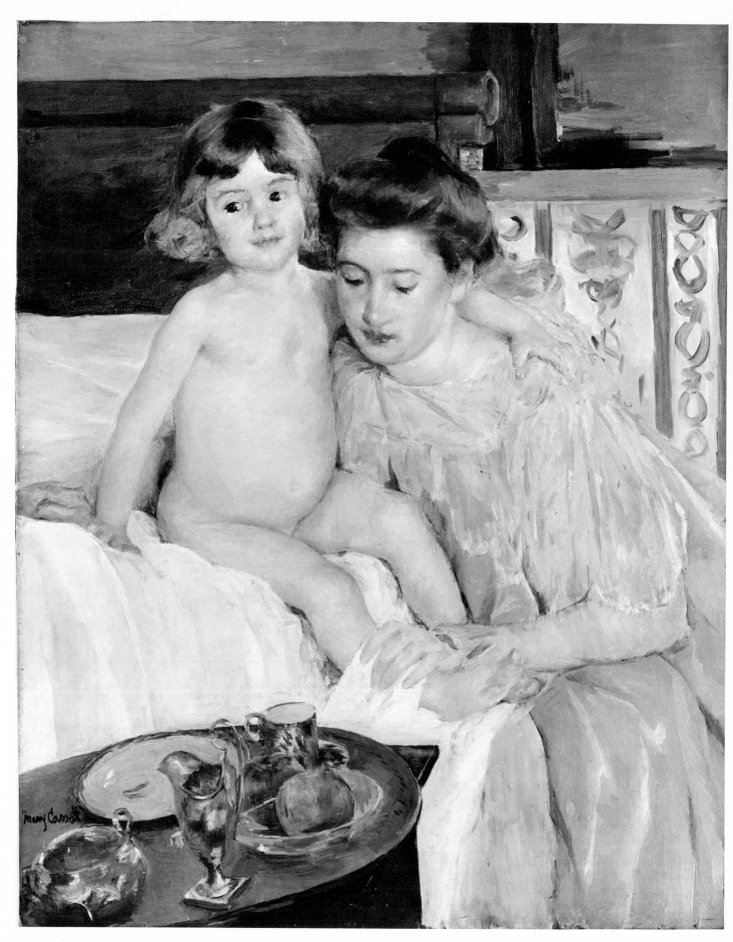

63 BABY GETTING UP FROM HIS NAP

54   IN THE PARK

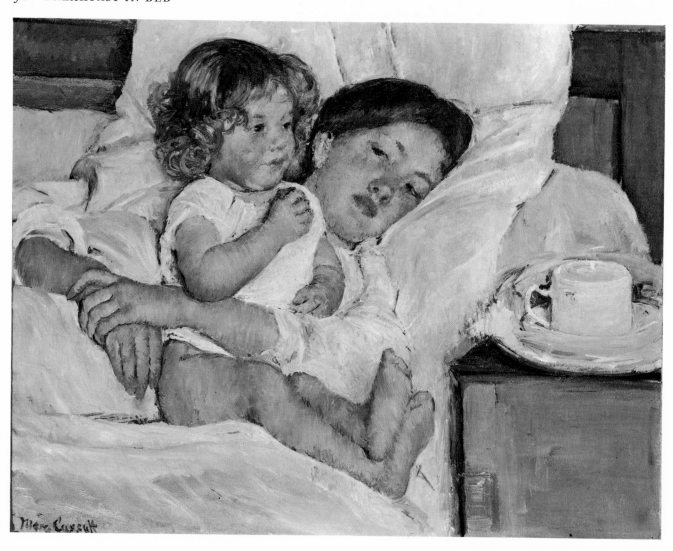

64 FAMILY GROUP READING

65 MOTHER AND DAUGHTER, BOTH WEARING LARGE HATS

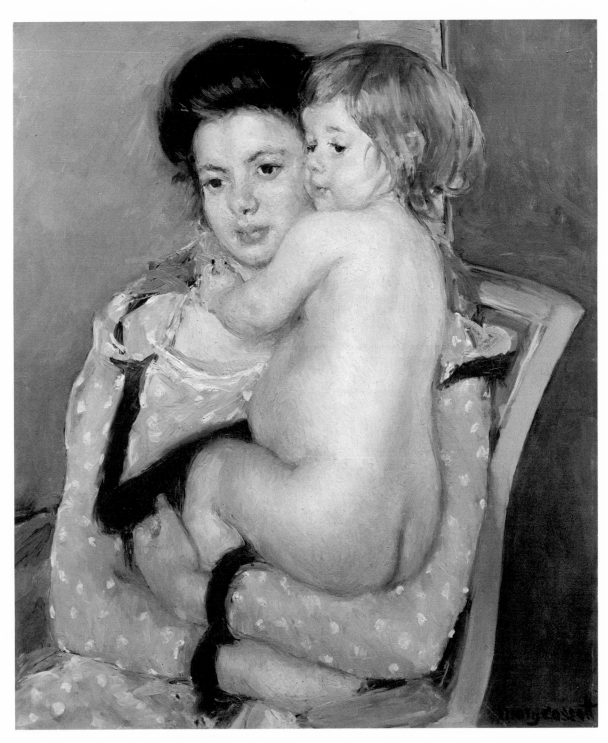

68 REINE LEFEBVRE HOLDING A NUDE BABY

69   YOUNG MOTHER SEWING

SIMONE IN A WHITE BONNET SEATED
WITH CLASPED HANDS (NO. 2)

62   PORTRAIT OF MME. A. F. AUDE AND HER TWO DAUGHTERS

76   THE CROCHET LESSON

72 SIMONE TALKING TO HER MOTHER

73   MOTHER AND CHILD IN A BOAT

75 ANTOINETTE AT HER DRESSING TABLE

79   FRANÇOISE SEWING (NO. I)

80   LITTLE GIRL HOLDING A DOLL

81 STUDY FOR "INTERIOR: ON THE SOFA"

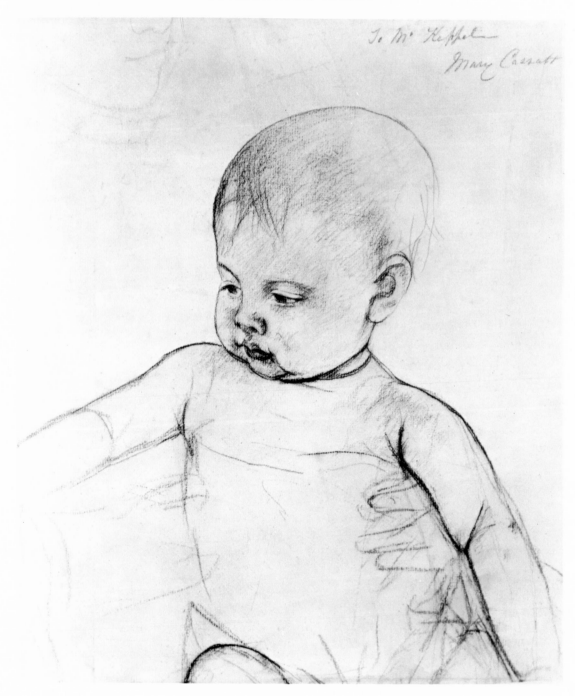

83   MOTHER PULLING ON BABY'S STOCKING

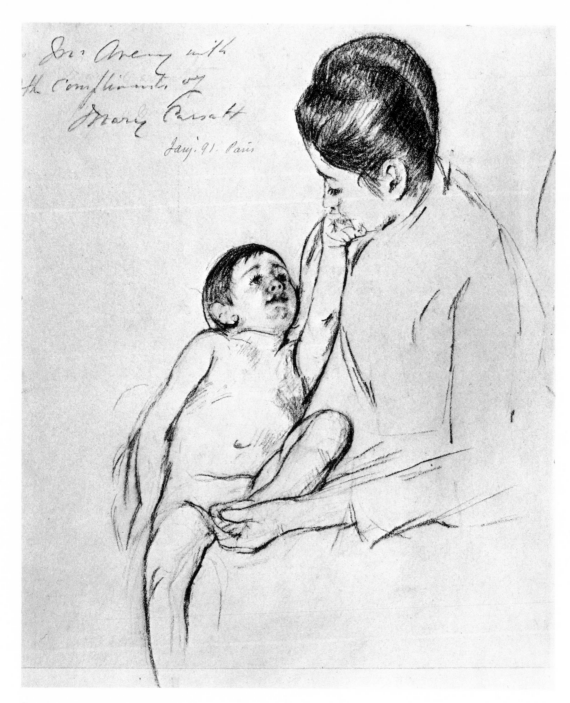

84 THE FIRST CARESS

87   STUDY FOR "GATHERING FRUIT"

89   PORTRAIT SKETCH OF MADAME FONTVEILLE (NO. 2)

90 PORTRAIT OF HERBERT JACOBY

BIOGRAPHICAL NOTES / BIBLIOGRAPHY

1844	Born, May 22, Allegheny City (now a part of Pittsburgh), Pennsylvania—the third child of Mr. and Mrs. Robert S. Cassatt.
1851–1858	Lived in Europe with her family in Paris, Heidelberg, and Darmstadt.
1858–1867	Lived in Philadelphia with her family.
1861–1865	Studied at the Pennsylvania Academy of Fine Arts.
1866	Went to Paris with her mother.
1867	Went to France with another Academy student to sketch and paint.
1870–1871	Came home to Philadelphia, because of the Franco-Prussian War.
1872	Went to Parma, Italy. Sent her first painting to the Paris Salon, *On the Balcony*.
1873	Went to Seville, from where she sent her second entry to the Salon, and then on to Belgium and Holland and finally to Paris again.
1874	Sent her third painting to the Salon. Visited Rome—sent her first two Salon entries to the National Academy of Design, New York.
1877	Her parents and her older sister, Lydia, came to Paris to live with her. Degas invited her to join the Impressionists.
1879	Sent two Impressionist paintings to the Society of American Artists (probably the first to be shown in America).
1879–1880	Worked very hard preparing prints to be published in *Le Jour et La Nuit*, a journal, never published, which Degas planned to launch.
1879, 1880, 1881, 1886	Exhibited paintings in the fourth, fifth, sixth, and eighth Impressionist Exhibitions.
1880	Brother Alexander Cassatt brought his family for a visit and she charmed his children into posing for her.
1882	Her sister Lydia died on November 7.
1887	The family moved to the apartment and studio at 10 rue Marignan, Paris, which she kept for the rest of her life.
1890	She visited the great Japanese print exhibition in Paris with Degas.
1890–1891	For the summer and fall, rented Château Bachivillers on the Oise. Set up her etching press there and worked on the set of 10 color prints with the help of the printer Leroy who came out from Paris to help her run them through the press.

1891	On June 10, her first one-man show opened at Durand-Ruel's, including the set of 10 color prints as well as 2 oils and 2 pastels. Her father died on December 9.
1892	Mrs. Potter Palmer commissioned her to do a large mural for the Woman's Building of the World's Columbian Exposition at Chicago. She completed it at Château Bachivillers.
1893	A larger one-man show at Durand-Ruel's, Paris, altogether 98 items. She bought the Château Beaufresne, at Mesnil-Theribus, Oise, her summer home for the rest of her life.
1895	A large one-man show similar to the 1893 one at Durand-Ruel's, Paris, held at their New York branch. Her mother died on December 21.
1898–1899	Her first visit back to America since settling in Paris in 1874.
1901	Trip with the Havemeyers to Italy and Spain encouraging them to buy El Grecos and other great paintings now in the Metropolitan Museum.
1904	Made a Chevalier of the Legion of Honor.
1905	Competed for a mural for the new capitol at Harrisburg, Pennsylvania but withdrew upon hearing of graft.
1906	Death of her brother Alexander who had been President of the Pennsylvania Railroad.
1908–1909	Last visit to America.
1910–1911	Stopped working on her drypoints since the shine of the copper hurt her eyes. Went to Egypt with her brother Gardner Cassatt and his family.
1911–1912	Nervous breakdown and illness after brother Gardner's death.
1912	First operation for cataracts on both eyes.
1914	Awarded Gold Medal of Honor by Pennsylvania Academy. Stopped painting due to blindness.
1914–1918	During First World War spent most of the time in Grasse, on the Riviera.
1926	Died at Château Beaufresne on June 14.

Beurdeley, Yveling Rambaud. "Mary Cassatt," *L'Art dans les Deux Mondes*, no. 1 (November 22, 1890), p. 7.

Biddle, George. "Some Memories of Mary Cassatt," *The Arts*, vol. X (August 1926), pp. 107–11.

Breeskin, Adelyn D. *The Graphic Work of Mary Cassatt, a catalogue raisonné*. New York, 1948.

Breuning, Margaret. *Mary Cassatt*. New York, 1944.

Carson, Julia M. H. *Mary Cassatt*. New York, 1966.

Cary, Elisabeth Luther. "The Art of Mary Cassatt," *The Scrip*, vol. I, no. 1 (October 1905), pp. 1–5.

Geffroy, Gustave. "Femmes artistes—un peintre de l'enfance: Mary Cassatt," *Les Modes*, vol. 4 (February 1904), pp. 4–11.

Grafly, Dorothy. "In Retrospect—Mary Cassatt," *American Magazine of Art*, vol. XVIII (June 1927), pp. 305–12.

Havemeyer, Louisine W. "The Cassatt Exhibition," *The Pennsylvania Museum Bulletin*, vol. XXII, no. 113 (May 1927), pp. 373–82.

_____. *Sixteen to Sixty, Memoirs of a Collector*, New York, 1961.

Ivins, William M. Jr. "New Exhibition in the Print Galleries; Prints by Mary Cassatt," *Bulletin of the Metropolitan Museum of Art*, vol. XXII, no. 1 (January 1927), pp. 8–10.

Kysela, S. J., John D. "Mary Cassatt's Mystery Mural and the World's Fair of 1893," *Art Quarterly*, vol. 29, no. 2 (1966), pp. 129–145.

McChesney, Clara. "Mary Cassatt and Her Work," *Arts and Decoration*, vol. III (June 1913), pp. 265–67.

Mauclair, Camille. "Un peintre de l'enfance, Miss Mary Cassatt," *L'Art Décoratif*, vol. VII, no. 47, (August 1902), pp. 177–85.

Mellerio, André. "Mary Cassatt," *L'Art et les Artistes*, vol. 12 (November 1910), pp. 69–75.

Ségard, Achille. *Mary Cassatt: un peintre des enfants et des mères*, Paris, 1913.

Sweet, Frederick A. "A Château in the Country," *The Art Quarterly*, vol. XXI, no. 2 (Summer 1958), pp. 202–15.

_____. *Miss Mary Cassatt: Impressionist from Pennsylvania*. Norman, Oklahoma, 1966.

Walton, William. "Miss Mary Cassatt," *Scribner's Magazine*, vol. XIX, no. 3 (March 1896), pp. 353–61.

Watson, Forbes. *Mary Cassatt*, New York, 1932.